Book 23—Teaching

The Greatest Commandments

Written by Anne de Graaf

Illustrated by José Pérez Montero

Family Time Bible Stories

Standard Publishing

Teaching-The Greatest Commandments

Matthew 18; Luke 9—11, 13—15, 17; John 7—11

About the Greatest Commandments

As Jesus travels through Israel, healing and helping, more and more people find themselves drawn to His teaching. Many do not know who He is. Many more do not want to know. Only a few open their minds and hearts to the knowledge that Jesus is the Son of God.

In all that He says and does, Jesus shows a new way of living. It is the kingdom of God, open to all who believe Jesus and ask Him to forgive them for their sins.

There are two great commandments in the kingdom of God. The first is, "Love the Lord your God with all your heart and with all your soul and with all your mind." The second is, "Love your neighbor as yourself."

When Jesus tells stories about how people should live, He is teaching about these commandments. Everything Jesus does from the way He brings one of His best friends back from the dead to how He defies His enemies and heals on the Sabbath shows how important it is to love.

Just a few days before He is killed, Jesus will talk to His enemies about these commandments. But long before that He is already showing others what it really means to love God and to love others.

LOVE YOUR NEIGHBOR
Forgive Again

Matthew 18:21-35

Peter asked Jesus how many times he should forgive someone who hurts him. To answer Peter's question, Jesus told this story.

"There once was a king who wanted to have all the money owed to him by his slaves. One slave owed the king so much money, there was no way he would ever be able to pay it back. So the king ordered the slave to be sold, along with his wife and children.

"The slave fell on his knees and begged, 'Just give me some time, and I promise I'll pay back everything!'

"The king felt sorry for his slave and said he did not have to pay back anything at all. But then the slave went out and found a fellow slave who owed him a small amount. 'Pay up, or else!' he shouted.

"The fellow slave begged for more time, but the first slave would not listen. He had the man thrown into prison.

"When news of the first slave's selfishness reached the king, he was very angry. He called the slave to him.

"'You wicked slave! I said you did not have to pay me back at all. You should have shown the same mercy to others.' And the king put the wicked slave in prison."

Jesus said that is how God will treat us if we do not forgive each other from our hearts.

4

The Seventy Sent Out

Luke 10:1-24

Jesus chose seventy of His disciples and sent them out in pairs. He told them to go ahead of Him into the towns and places He planned to go. He said there were many people who would turn their lives around and follow His teachings, but more people were needed to spread the word.

Jesus warned these seventy disciples that they would not have an easy job. "Don't carry any money with you and don't waste any time along the way. Stay at the homes of good men. Preach about the kingdom of God and heal the sick.

"If any town turns you away, they will be judged by God. Those who refuse me turn away the one who sent me!"

Later, when the seventy disciples returned, they were full of exciting stories. "Lord, even the evil spirits obey us when we speak Your name!"

Jesus was full of joy. "Thank You Father. You've hidden these things from the people who think they are so wise, and shown them to those with faith like little children!"

The Healed Leper

Luke 17:11-16

As Jesus came to a certain village, ten lepers stood waiting to meet Him. They wore hoods over their heads and scarves across their faces. They were covered from head to toe, so no one would have to look at their awful sores.

Because they were lepers, they were not allowed to stand near the road. But even from a distance they could call out, "Jesus! Teacher! Have mercy on us!"

Jesus stopped. He knew how desperate the lepers felt. They had no hope of leading normal lives.

Jesus said to them, "Go and show yourselves to the priests." This was another way of telling the lepers they were healed! Only people who had been healed were supposed to go to the priests.

The men did as Jesus told them. As they began to walk to see the priests, they felt something happen in their bodies. One man pulled his sleeve up and saw the skin actually growing back healthy, before his own eyes.

He shouted, "Praise God! Praise the Lord God Almighty! I have been healed! I am whole!"

Then he turned around, and as fast as he could, ran straight back to where Jesus was. He fell at Jesus' feet and cried, "Thank You, oh, thank You!"

Why Not Say Thank-You?

Luke 17:17-19

The leper who ran back to thank Jesus for healing him was a Samaritan.

Samaritans were a tribe of people who had been fighting with the Jews for hundreds of years.

Jesus looked at the man who held onto His feet so tightly and kept singing out his thanks to God. He said, "But weren't there ten who were healed? Where are the other nine? Is the only man to give glory to God this foreigner?"

Then Jesus told the man, "Get up and go your way. Your faith has made you well."

Why did only one man return? It could be that the other nine did not come back and say thank you for the same reasons people do not thank God for their blessings today.

Perhaps one leper simply forgot.

Another may have been too shy. Maybe one was too proud, since saying thank you meant he admitted he could not heal himself.

Perhaps another leper was so excited about being healed, he lost his way and could not find Jesus again. It could be that one was too busy. There were many people he wanted to tell about his being healed, and there was a lot of living to catch up on.

One leper may not have come back to say thank you because the priest told him he did not have to, and this man always did what others told him, without thinking for himself. The seventh leper may not have said thank you because he did not understand what had happened to him. It just did not make sense. It wasn't possible for a leper to be healed, yet he had been! He was so overwhelmed by the miracle, he forgot all about Jesus.

The eighth leper may not have gone back to see Jesus because he simply saw no reason to. He had never said thank you to anyone for anything and saw no reason to start.

And perhaps the last leper was just so filled with happiness and devotion to the God that it never even occurred to him to return to the one who had done this for him.

Only one leper of the ten saw how Jesus heals the whole person, as well as the body. As happens so often, the others took the gift God gave them for granted. God gives us what we need—food, shelter, clothing, health. How often do we thank Him?

WHERE DO WE STAND?

The Crowds Are Confused

John 7:10-53

Jesus went to Jerusalem for the Feast of Tabernacles. He entered the city secretly, after everyone else had already gone to the feast.

Everywhere He went, Jesus heard the crowds whispering about Him. "Where is Jesus?" "I thought He would be here. Have you heard of all the miracles He has done?"

"Who is this Jesus, anyway? Have you seen Him?"

The people were not the only ones looking for Jesus. His enemies, the religious leaders, also wanted to find Him. They did not understand who Jesus was, and they did not like the power He had over the people.

Jesus went into the temple to teach. The people who heard Him were amazed at His wisdom. The religious leaders said, "How can He preach so well, when He never went to any of the special schools?"

Jesus said, "This teaching isn't mine. It comes from God, who sent me. Why are you trying to kill me?"

"Are You crazy?" the people shouted back. "No one wants to kill You!" But Jesus looked straight at the Pharisees, the religious leaders. He knew they hated Him.

But these teachers of the Jewish law were afraid if they did arrest Jesus, the crowds would get angry.

Many of the people did believe Jesus was the Messiah, but others said, "We know Jesus did not come from Bethlehem, and that is where the Messiah is supposed to come from. Jesus comes from Galilee." But they did not know Jesus had indeed been born in Bethlehem.

The religious leaders sent guards from the temple to arrest Jesus, but the guards came back without Him. "No one ever spoke the way He does," they told the leaders.

Then Nicodemus, a Pharisee who believed in Jesus, questioned the other leaders. "Don't you think you should wait? Our law says we can't condemn Jesus without a trial."

The other men turned on him. "Whose side are you on? Look and see for yourself. The Scriptures don't say anything about a prophet coming from Galilee."

A Second Chance

John 8:1-11

On one of the last mornings of the Feast of Tabernacles, Jesus went to the temple early in the morning and began to teach.

The religious leaders dragged a woman over to Him. She sobbed with fear as the men stood her in front of everyone.

"Teacher," they said. "This married woman was found sleeping with a man who is not her husband. The laws Moses gave us say she should be killed by stoning. What do You say?"

Jesus did not answer them. Instead, He bent down and wrote in the dust.

"Well?" the Pharisees asked. "What do You think we should do with her?"

Jesus stood up. "Let the person who has never done anything wrong be the first to throw a stone at her." Then He stooped down and wrote in the dust again.

Everyone listening knew he had done many wrong things, so one by one, the people snuck away. The older people left first. No one said a word. In the end, Jesus was left alone with the woman.

"Woman," Jesus said. "Where are they? Didn't anyone throw a stone at you?"

She raised her head and looked around. "No one, Lord," she said.

Jesus said, "Then I will not condemn you, either. But leave your sinful ways."

The woman went away, filled with wonder at the second chance she had been given.

Where Did He Come From?

John 8:15-59

The time had come for Jesus to tell the people who He was and where He had come from. "The Father in Heaven sent me. And it is back to Him that I will go, when I leave here.

"I am the Son of Man. And everything I say is what the Father has told me to say. He has not left me alone. I always do what He wants."

The religious leaders grew angrier and angrier as Jesus said these things. But when the people in the crowd heard Him, many came to believe in Him. To these people, then, Jesus said, "If you hold on to what I have taught, then you are truly my disciples. You will know the truth, and the truth will set you free."

"But we are not slaves," the people said.

"Every person is a slave to the wrong things he does," Jesus said. He told them He could give them true freedom.

Then Jesus said that those who follow Him would never die.

But again the religious leaders grew angry. "You are crazy!" they shouted at Him. They did not understand that Jesus was talking about the life after death, in Heaven. "Abraham died, and You are not greater than Abraham," they shouted.

Then Jesus told them He had existed even before Abraham was born.

And at that, the religious leaders picked up stones because they wanted to kill Him. But Jesus hid himself, and left the temple without them even seeing Him.

Three Men

Luke 10:25-37

A man who had spent years studying the law wanted to test Jesus. "Teacher, how do I get to Heaven?" he asked.

"What does the law say?" Jesus asked.

The man answered, "Love God completely and love your neighbor as yourself."

"Do that and you will live," Jesus said.

But the man asked, "Who is my neighbor?"

Jesus answered with this story. "There once was a man walking from Jerusalem to Jericho. Suddenly, robbers jumped out of nowhere. They beat him up and stole everything he had, even his clothes. They left him there, half dead.

"Along came a priest. When he saw the man, he crossed to the other side of the road and passed by him as quickly as he could. 'I don't want to get involved,' he thought to himself.

"Along came a religious leader, one who preached the laws of Moses. When he saw the man, he also crossed to the other side of the road and passed him by.

"Then came a Samaritan. Even though the man who lay in the dirt was a Jew, and Samaritans and Jews have been enemies for hundreds of years, the Samaritan came over to him. He cleaned and bandaged the man's wounds. Then he carried the man and put him onto his own donkey and brought him into town, to an inn, and cared for him there.

"The next day, the Samaritan gave money to the innkeeper and said, 'Spend what you need to take good care of him until he is strong. If you spend more than this, I will repay you.'

"Which one of these three was a neighbor to the man who was robbed?" asked Jesus.

"The one who was kind," the lawyer replied.

"Go and be like him," Jesus said.

FRIENDS OF JESUS
Martha and Mary

Luke 10:38-42

Jesus often stopped in the village of Bethany, where Martha, Mary, and their brother, Lazarus, lived. At those times, He went to their home to rest and get away from all the crowds. During one of His visits, Martha learned a very important lesson.

Jesus was relaxing in the main room, talking to Mary. Martha was very excited that Jesus was visiting them, and she wanted everything to be just right. There was only one problem. Martha could not possibly do all the work by herself.

She rushed about, gathering herbs and vegetables from the garden, cleaning and cooking. Then she noticed that Mary was doing nothing at all. Mary sat at Jesus' feet, listening to all He said.

Martha went to Jesus and complained. "Lord," she said, "don't You care that my sister has left me to do all the serving alone? Tell her to help me!"

But Jesus answered, "Martha, Martha, you are worried and bothered about so many things. Only one thing is needed. Mary wants to hear what I teach. She has chosen what is best and it won't be taken away from her.

Did Martha nod and settle onto the floor, next to her sister, so they could listen to Jesus together? The Bible doesn't tell us. But we can hope that from then on, Martha never made working for Jesus more important than spending time getting to know Him. That's a lesson all followers of Jesus should remember.

The Friend at Midnight

Luke 11:5-13

Jesus told this story about prayer.

"There once was a man who came and knocked on the door of his friend at midnight. 'What do you want?' his friend yelled from inside the house. 'What do you want? I need to borrow three loaves of bread,' said the man. 'Someone has come to visit me, but I haven't got any food!'

"His friend called back, 'Don't bother me about that! The door is shut and my family's already asleep. I can't get up and give you anything.'

"But the man who needed the extra bread kept right on knocking and shouting.

"Finally, his friend did open the door, because the man would not stop

To See

John 9:1-23

Jesus saw a man who had been born blind. He had to beg for a living. The disciples asked Jesus if the man's blindness was a punishment from God.

"No," said Jesus. "He was born blind so the power of God can be shown right now."

Then Jesus said, "While I am in the world, I am the light of the world." He spit into the dust, made some mud, and then put the mud over the blind man's eyes. "Go and wash your eyes in the pool of Siloam," He said.

The man did so, and he could see! But Jesus was already gone, so the man went home.

The people who had known the blind man all his life watched him and said, "Is this really the same man who used to sit over there and beg?"

He said over and over again, "Yes, yes, I'm the one."

"Well, how were your eyes opened?" they asked. When he told them what had happened, they wanted to know where Jesus was.

"I don't know," said the man.

So the people brought him to the Pharisees. When they heard the story, some believed Jesus was a holy man sent from God. "Who else could heal a man blind from birth?" they asked.

The man's parents were called, to find out if the man really had been blind since birth.

"How was your son healed?" the Pharisees asked. But the parents were

knocking and asking."

Jesus explained that people who pray to God are like the man who stood outside his friend's house. "Keep asking, and it will be given to you. Keep looking and you will find. Keep knocking and the door will be opened to you."

"Suppose one of you fathers is asked by his son for a fish. Would you give him a snake instead?" Jesus asked. "God knows even more how to give good things to His children."

afraid. The Pharisees had said that anyone who called Jesus the Messiah would not be allowed to worship in the synagogue.

So the parents just said, "Ask our son. He's old enough to answer for himself."

Who Was Blind?

John 9:24-41

The Pharisees asked the man again, "Who healed you? We know it couldn't have been Jesus."

"I don't know who it was," he said. "All I know is, I was blind and now I see!"

"But what did He do to you? How did He open your eyes?"

"I told you! Weren't you listening? Do you want to hear the story again

because you believe in Him, like I do?"

This made the Pharisees very angry. "We don't even know where he comes from," they said."

The man laughed. "Never has anyone else been able to heal a man who was blind from birth, a man like me. God hears those who do His will. This man must be from God or He could do nothing."

The religious leaders did not want to hear that Jesus was from God. They threw the man out and told him he could never worship in the synagogue again.

Later Jesus found the man. "Do you believe in the Son of Man?" Jesus asked him.

"I know that voice," thought the man, and he said, "Who is He, that I may believe in Him?"

Jesus answered, "You have both seen and heard Him now."

The man fell to his knees and worshiped Jesus. "Lord, I believe," he said.

Jesus said, "I came here so the blind can see, and those who see will become blind."

Some of the Pharisees nearby said, "But we're not blind."

Jesus said, "Because you think you see, you're blind." Because their minds were closed, they could not see Him as the Son of God.

JESUS SAYS, "I AM..."
The Good Shepherd

John 10:21

"I am the Good Shepherd," Jesus said. He told a story to explain why He called himself that.

"The shepherd stands at the gate of the sheep pen. He knows which sheep are his own and lets his sheep pass through the gate to the pasture. He keeps away all the wild animals.

"The good shepherd does anything he can to take care of his sheep. He would even die to save them. Because the sheep are his, he does not run away when a wolf comes, leaving his sheep to be killed. That's what someone who is hired for the job might do.

"I am the Good Shepherd. I know my own and they know me. I will lay down my life for those who follow me."

"What kind of person talks like He does?" the Jewish leaders asked each other. "He has a demon and he is crazy," some said. Why do you listen to Him?"

But others said, "These aren't the sayings of a crazy person. After all, He opened the eyes of a blind man, remember?"

21

Man or God?

John 10:22-42

Later, Jesus went back to Jerusalem. While He was walking by the same place in Jerusalem where Solomon's temple had stood, the Jewish leaders came and blocked His way. "Enough of this!" they said. "Tell us who You really are! If You are the Christ, then just say so! Tell us plainly!"

Jesus answered them, "I told you, and you didn't believe me. Think of the miracles I have done in my Father's name.

"You don't believe because you are not my sheep. My sheep hear my voice. I know them, and they follow me. My sheep will never die. My Father has given them to me. My Father is God. We are the same person."

According to Jewish law, to pretend to be God was a severe crime. The punishment was death.

The Jews picked up stones to throw at Jesus.

But Jesus said, "Are you throwing stones at me because of a miracle I did?"

"No!" the leaders shouted. "It is because You, who are only human, want people to think You're as good as God!"

Jesus said, "If I don't do the works of my Father, then don't believe me. But if I do what He does, believe the miracles, and know that the Father is in me, and I am in the Father."

This was too much for the Jews. They tried to seize Him, but He escaped.

Lazarus Is Dead

John 11:1-28

After the religious leaders tried to stone Jesus, He left the city and went into the countryside. While He was there, He got a message from Mary and Martha: "Our brother Lazarus is very sick."

When Jesus heard this, He said, "This sickness has a purpose. It won't end in death." Instead of going straight to Bethany to help Lazarus, Jesus waited two days. Then He said, "Now we will go. Our friend Lazarus has fallen asleep. I will wake him up."

"But Teacher, if Lazarus is asleep, he can wake up by himself," the disciples said.

Jesus said softly, "Lazarus is dead, and I am glad we weren't there earlier because now your trust in me will grow."

The disciples did not know what to think, so they quietly followed Jesus to Bethany. When they arrived, they discovered that Lazarus had been buried four days before.

Martha, met Jesus on His way into the village. "Oh, Lord," she said, "if You had been here, my brother would not have died. But I know that whatever You ask of God, He gives You."

Jesus told her Lazarus would rise again. Martha said, "I know he will rise again when You come back on the last day of the world."

Jesus said, "He who believes in me will never die. Do you believe this?"

"Yes, Lord. You are the Christ, the Son of God." Then she went to get her sister, Mary.

24

Lazarus Lives

John 11:29-46

Martha's home was filled with friends, all mourning the death of Lazarus. She went to Mary and said, "The Teacher is here, and He wants to see you."

Mary quickly got up and followed Martha. When she saw Jesus, she fell at His feet, weeping. "Lord, if You had been here, he would not have died."

The friends of the family had followed Mary outside, thinking she was going to where Lazarus was buried. They all cried, men and women alike. When Jesus saw how sad they were, He was deeply moved in spirit.

"Where have you laid him?" He asked. They led Him toward a cave with a large stone blocking the way.

Jesus wept.

At the tomb He said, "Take the stone away."

"But Lord, he has been dead four days," said Martha. "There will be a very bad smell."

But Jesus said, "Remember, Martha. I said if you believed, you would see the glory of God."

So they did as Jesus asked. Once the cave was opened, Jesus gave thanks to God. Then He said in a loud voice, "Lazarus, come out!"

Out of the cave, wrapped with cloths, came Lazarus. "Unbind him, and let him go," said Jesus.

Mary and Martha rushed forward, hardly daring to hope that inside the white cloths their beloved brother could be alive. When they had unwrapped him, the crowd cried out and there was even more weeping than before. It was Lazarus, alive!

Many people put their faith in Jesus that day. But others went to the Pharisees, and told them what Jesus had done.

To Heal or Not to Heal

Luke 13:10-17

When He was teaching in a synagogue Jesus saw a woman who could not stand up straight. She had been hunched over for eighteen years because of an evil spirit.

Jesus called her forward and said, "Woman, you are freed from your sickness." Then He laid His hands on her, and suddenly she stood up straight and began praising God.

But the synagogue ruler thought that because it was the Sabbath, Jesus should not have healed her. No Jews were allowed to work on the day of rest.

Jesus told them healing was not work. He grew angry. "You hypocrites! You all untie your ox or donkey and lead it to water on the Sabbath. Well, is this daughter of Abraham, one of God's own chosen people, better or worse than an ox? She has been bound for eighteen years. Why shouldn't she be set free on the Sabbath day?"

When all the people heard Jesus' answer, they were delighted! Jesus' enemies were humiliated.

THE KINGDOM OF GOD
A Place in Heaven

Luke 13:23-30

Someone asked Jesus how many people would get to go to Heaven.

Jesus said, "Many will try to enter, but they will not be able to get in."

He told them a story about themselves. "Once the owner of the house gets up and shuts the door, you will knock and shout, saying, 'Lord, let us in!'

"Then He will answer, 'But I don't even know where you come from.'

"Some may say, 'Oh, I knew Jesus. I ate and drank with Him and He taught in my village.'

"But the owner will say, 'Away from me, you evildoers!'" It won't be enough just to claim to know God. We must allow Jesus to change our lives. That is the way into the kingdom of heaven.

Jesus said that following Him is like going through a narrow door. It means putting God first and loving others. This is different than the way most people live.

Jesus said that people would come from all over the world to take their places at the table in the kingdom of God. And some who are not important on earth will be first in the kingdom of Heaven, and some who are important now will come last.

An Ox in the Well

Luke 14:1-6

The Pharisees set a trap for Jesus. It happened on a Sabbath day, when no Jews were supposed to work.

Jesus had gone to eat at the home of one of the Pharisees. A very sick man had been invited too. The Pharisees wanted to see if Jesus would heal the man on the Sabbath day of rest. If He did, they could say He had broken the law again.

Jesus asked them, "Is it against the law to make sick people better on the Sabbath, or not?"

But the Pharisees would not answer. So Jesus reached out to the sick man and healed him. Then Jesus sent him away.

The Pharisees thought, "Ah, now we have Him!"

But Jesus said, "Which one of you has a son or an ox? If he fell into a well on the day of rest, which of you would not rush to pull him out as quickly as possible?"

Not one of the Pharisees would answer Jesus' question. Of course, they all knew they would save their ox or their son if he fell into a well. But to tell Jesus this would be the same as saying Jesus was right to heal the sick man on the Sabbath.

The Dinner Guests

Luke 14:7-24

Later, Jesus saw that the guests at the Pharisee's house were choosing the seats of honor at the table. So He told this story.

"At a wedding feast, nobody takes the place of honor without being invited to sit there. The host might come and tell him to give his seat to a more important guest. It is better to take the last place. That way the host can come and say, 'Friend, come closer to the seat of honor.'"

While they were eating, Jesus told them another story. "A certain man was giving a big dinner. He invited many people. But when it came time for the dinner, none of the guests showed up. Instead, they all made excuses.

"So the man told his servant, 'Go out into the streets then. Bring the poor, the crippled, the lame and the blind to me. That way my house will be filled. And I tell you, none of those men who were invited first will ever taste any of my food!'"

That is how it will be in the kingdom of Heaven. Anyone who thinks he is already a good person and does not need God won't be able to enter the kingdom, even though he has been invited.

29

How Much Does It Cost?

Luke 14:25-33

Why did Jesus teach that following Him is like going through a narrow door, and that not many people would find the way? Was it because it is too hard to find the way?

No. It was because, like the guests who were invited to dinner, some choose not to follow the way. Some choose not to follow Jesus because the price is too high. Just what is that price? One day, Jesus talked about what it costs to follow Him.

"If anyone comes to me, He said, he must love me more than anyone else. His love for me must be so great that, by comparison, it looks like he loves no one else.

"Before you set out to follow me, count the cost. No one of you can become my disciple unless he is willing to give up everything in life. This means loving me more than all that you own."

To follow Jesus means to be ready to do whatever He asks, to obey Him. Jesus wanted His disciples to love Him above all else. That is what He asks of us as well.

The Lost Sheep and the Lost Coin

Luke 15:1-10

God treasures every child, every man, and every woman. He would like nothing better than for everyone to be saved.

Jesus told two stories about how much every person is worth to God. The first story was about a lost sheep.

Jesus asked, "If you had a hundred sheep and lost one of them, wouldn't you go after the one that was lost? And when it was found, wouldn't you carry it back to the flock and call your friends together? 'I have found my lost sheep,' you would say.

"In the same way, there will be more joy in Heaven over one sinner who turns away from his sins than over ninety-nine people who are already good."

The second story was about a woman who lost a coin worth an entire day's work. Jesus said, "If a woman has ten coins and loses one, won't she light a lamp and sweep the house, looking everywhere until she finds it?

"And when she has found it, she will call together her friends and say, 'Be happy with me! I finally found my lost coin!'

"In the same way," Jesus said, "the angels smile and sing whenever one person turns away from his sins."

Old Testament

New Testament